The CRAF-E⁴ Family Engagement Model

The CRAF-E⁴ Family Engagement Model

Building Practitioners' Competence to Work with Diverse Families

Iheoma U. Iruka, Ph.D.

Stephanie M. Curenton, Ph.D.

Winnie A. I. Eke, Ph.D.

ELSEVIER

AMSTERDAM • BOSTON • HEIDELBERG • LONDON
NEW YORK • OXFORD • PARIS • SAN DIEGO
SAN FRANCISCO • SINGAPORE • SYDNEY • TOKYO

Academic Press is an imprint of Elsevier

Academic Press is an imprint of Elsevier
32 Jamestown Road, London NW1 7BY, UK
The Boulevard, Langford Lane, Kidlington, Oxford, OX5 1GB, UK
Radarweg 29, PO Box 211, 1000 AE Amsterdam, The Netherlands
225 Wyman Street, Waltham, MA 02451, USA
525 B Street, Suite 1900, San Diego, CA 92101-4495, USA

British Library Cataloguing-in-Publication Data
A catalogue record for this book is available from the British Library

Library of Congress Cataloging-in-Publication Data
A catalog record for this book is available from the Library of Congress

ISBN: 978-0-12-410415-0

For information on all Academic Press publications
visit our website at **store.elsevier.com**

This book has been manufactured using Print On Demand technology. Each copy is produced to order
and is limited to black ink. The online version of this book will show color figures where appropriate.

ELSEVIER Book Aid International **Working together
to grow libraries in
developing countries**

www.elsevier.com • www.bookaid.org

CONTENTS

INTRODUCTION

The purpose of this book is to share strategies for how school-based practitioners (such as teachers, clinicians, social workers, speech-language pathologist (SLP), program directors and/or school administrators) working in early education settings with children from age 0 to 8 can successfully work with racially and ethnically diverse families (e.g., Blacks/African Americans, Hispanic/Latinos, Whites, or any other racial/ethnic category used in the United States). In this book, *diversity* is used to describe the wide variety of cultural, linguistic, economic, national, and socio-political differences represented among racial and ethnic minority families. Because our definition of diversity is so broad, in our discussions we attempt to provide enough specific detail that you will begin to see children and families occupying the multiple identities that are present in real life, rather than simply their larger racial or ethnic categories. For example, we might describe an SLP as an English-speaking monolingual Puerto Rican living in New York City, or a social worker as a Chinese and English bilingual clinician living in a rural community in Iowa. We believe this level of specificity captures the layers of multiple identities that characterize racial and ethnic minority people living within this country. Culturally responsive, anti-bias strategies are needed to engage the wide variety of diverse children and families who are now entering our education system. In order to more successfully partner with these diverse families, we suggest a family engagement model that is based on a culturally responsive, anti-biased framework characterized by the principles of multicultural education (see Curenton & Iruka, 2013), the **CRAF-E⁴**.

CHAPTER 1

CRAF-E^4: Increasing the Capacity and Engagement of Diverse Families

1.1 DESCRIPTION OF THE CRAF-E^4

Our culturally responsive, antibiased framework for family engagement is called the **CRAF-E^4**, the Culturally Responsive, Anti-bias Framework of Expectation, Education, Exploration, and Empowerment. This framework was designed to help early childhood practitioner's engage with racially and ethnically diverse families in a manner that adopts the principles of cultural responsiveness and antibias. **Culturally responsive, antibias family engagement** incorporates the cultural knowledge, experiences, and communication styles of diverse students and their families, and it acknowledges the social injustices, inequalities, and prejudices these families face.

In our model, **family engagement** is defined as the "relationship" the practitioner develops with a family, a relationship that encourages, and actively invites, family members to become involved in their child's education both inside and outside of the classroom. Family engagement is purposefully defined as a "relationship" in order to highlight the emotional underpinnings of the exchanges between teachers and family members; in addition, it is our view that it is the teacher's responsibility to repeatedly invite and encourage families to become involved. The National Association for the Education of Young Children's (NAEYC) *Engaging Diverse Families Project* (http://www.naeyc.org/familyengagement/about) explains that family engagement is based on the following principles:

Principle 1. Inviting families to participate in decision making and goal setting for their child.
Principle 2. Engaging families in two-way communication.
Principle 3. Engaging families in ways that are truly reciprocal.
Principle 4. Providing learning activities for the home and in the community.

The CRAF-E^4 Family Engagement Model. DOI: http://dx.doi.org/10.1016/B978-0-12-410415-0.00001-4

Principle 5. Inviting families to participate in program-level decisions and wider advocacy efforts
Principle 6. Implementing a comprehensive program-level system of family engagement.

Our framework will help practitioners accomplish the 4E's (Iruka, 2013):

- **"Expect"** families and students to do their best
- **"Educate"** families on how to support their children's optimal development
- **"Explore"** ways to partner with families and value their strengths
- **"Empower"** families to advocate on behalf of their child's education and well-being

Each of the 4E's is described in the following sections.

1.2 CRAF-4^E—IMPLICATIONS FOR PRACTICE

1.2.1 Expectation

The **CRAF-E^4** framework asks practitioners to raise their expectations of racial and ethnic minority children and families. All too often teachers, school administrators, or clinicians hold low expectations for these students and their families. Often people are not even consciously aware of these low expectations. Yet, such low expectations, regardless of whether they are explicitly stated or just implicitly acted out, have a major influence on how children feel about themselves and their performance. Educators often hold low expectations for minority families' engagement, especially low-income parents, at least as it concerns school-based activities (e.g., class visits, volunteering, and attending parent—teacher conferences); therefore, these low expectations might serve as an emotional barrier between teachers and family members.

Low expectations have been cited as a major contributing factor to the gap found between minority children's versus others' achievement, because such expectations undermine children's sense of competency and increase their sense of **learned helplessness** (McKown & Weinstein, 2008). Children develop a sense of learned helplessness when they repeatedly receive negative feedback or are repeatedly placed in a negative situation that is beyond their control and from which they cannot escape. Eventually, a child who experiences learned helplessness will stop trying to do better, meaning they will internalize the low expectations that people have of them.

Barriers often cited for the lack of family engagement are time, availability, stress, transportation, and child care. While real enough, these barriers are often used punitively to reinforce the expectations of limited family engagement, which in turn leads to more limited involvement. Thus, practitioners should foster a school culture in which parents are expected to be *intentionally and proactively* engaged in their child's learning and school experiences. It requires, for example, that schools assess the value of having parents coming into the school for activities and exploring alternative opportunities that support social networks and leadership roles.

Opportunities for Reflection from the Field

An employer-sponsored child care program has quarterly preschool open houses in which they invite parents in to learn more about the curriculum that is being taught in the classroom. These open houses are routinely offered at 4 pm on a workday; therefore, parents must leave work early in order to attend. The teacher, Mrs. Jones, has noticed that neither Sean's father, who is a high-level executive at the firm, never attends these open houses nor does Emily's mother who works in the cafeteria of the company. What are some potential challenges these families might be facing that prevent them from coming to the open houses? What can Mrs. Jones do to ensure these parents get the information they need about their children's education?

1.2.2 Education

Families are deeply knowledgeable about their children's strengths and weaknesses, and, with the right resources and supports in place, they can meet their children's needs. It is important that parents are educated on how to navigate the complex education institutions and system they are likely to encounter. Educating them on how to navigate these institutions will be for the benefit of their children. Parents need to learn how to advocate for such things as choosing a preschool that meets their young child's needs to deciding whether to test their 2nd grader for gifted and talented programs to seeking additional support for children who have special needs. This skill of advocacy and education can potentially be generalizable to all aspects of their lives where they may need support.

Early childhood education programs and schools often engage in partnerships with a variety of community and local agencies that, together, can help share information, encourage and support advocacy, and promote access to resources and networks. Shared data systems, such as the Early Childhood Data system (http://www.ecedata.org/files/2013%20State%20of%20States%27%20Early%20Childhood%20Data%20Systems.pdf) and other ongoing communication can help to ensure that families seeking information and support are connected not only to appropriate services and resources but also to each other, which helps to build critically important social capital and networks. For example, if one parent is known to have skills navigating special education services on behalf of her child, teachers might introduce her to another who is seeking assistance and advice on navigating a similar system for his child.

●●●

Opportunities for Reflection from the Field

Ms. Jane, a toddler teacher from a Montessori preschool in a small rural community, has a new student who enrolls. Brandon, the new child, has special needs in that he has mild physical disabilities due to cerebral palsy. Ms. Jane has prior experience working with toddlers with disabilities because another child in the classroom also has cerebral palsy, so Brandon's mother purposefully enrolled him with Ms. Jane. Because Brandon's family is new to the area, his mother has been depending on Ms. Jane for lots of information about doctors and social services that are available in the community. Ms. Jane does not always know the answers to these questions, but she believes the mother of the other student with cerebral palsy might be able to help. How can Ms. Jane go about introducing the two families? How can Ms. Jane find out more information herself to pass on to Brandon's mother?

1.2.3 Exploration

Minority families have a rich set of cultural practices and skills that need to be explored and valued when interacting with families. These cultural-based practices and skills can be referred to as **"funds of knowledge**

(FoKs)." In the context of education, **FoKs** consists of resources, cultural practices, and bodies of knowledge that families manipulate to survive, make ends meet, get ahead, and/or thrive (Hogg, 2011; Moll & Greenberg, 1990). Practitioners can call upon these "FoKs" when working with families as well as students; By using FoKs practitioners will be validating families' and students' experiences and knowledge and using these to scaffold the work with families (Hogg, 2011, p. 667).

One can identify families' FoKs through multiple approaches, including home visits or other opportunities that lead to conversations about and observations of families' routines and rituals. It is critical to approach families without judgment—so that the focus of the discussion can be about the many ways in which families can support their children's learning, success, unique talents, and contributions. To elicit the FoK of families, educators must be careful not to diminish the various activities, skills, and routines in which families engage, no matter how different they may be from their own. Educators should instead consider how what they learn may enhance their relationship with the child and family, as well as how their new knowledge could be integrated into classroom instruction, program activities, and events.

Programs should look to FoKs to unearth the skills and assets of parents and families. In addition to initial home visits, schools or centers can support targeted surveys, interviews or focus groups to help them better understand how they can build upon parents' goals for their child's education and to encourage and support their engagement. Programs should find ways to help parents and families meet the expectations for family engagement. Schools may find that, in order for parents to be fully engaged, they have to feel that they are making a difference in ways that make them valued partners and contributors. This perspective may lead to opportunities to invite parents to develop classroom lessons and activities based on their skills and talents; form parent–buddy or mentor programs; hold events at varying times and in alternative locations; and encourage parents to take on leadership roles in initiatives that schools may not be able to prioritize on their own, such as father–child engagement programs.

Opportunities for Reflection from the Field

A charter school that serves children from pre-K to grade 3 is interested in getting families to volunteer more around the school. The school principal decides to create a brief survey that asks parents what their skills, hobbies, and areas of expertise are. What sort of questions should be in this survey? What is the best way for the principal to follow up with families after getting the survey results?

1.2.4 Empowerment

The crux of our family engagement framework is to empower families to be appropriately equipped to face the challenges they will encounter in the education system. Family support programs are key to empowering families. Such family support programs should focus on empowering families within their life contexts and cultural environments a priority, ensuring that the skills they develop are transferable, create a sense of self-agency, and promote self-control. Family support programs identified as being the most effective for families and children focus on providing the families with the tools to achieve their goals as opposed to doing it for the family (Avellar, Paulsell, Sama-Miller, & Grosso, 2012). Home visiting programs, including the Nurse–Family Partnership, are examples of such support programs.

Empowering families is a process of building self-competence and self-sufficiency that requires programs to explore families' assets and capacities, educate them on issues around advocacy and networking, and hold high expectations about their role as parents in all aspects of their child's development. Empowering families does not mean "doing it" for the family—which may be easier in the short run but increasingly harmful in the long term. If, for example, a parent is seeking more information about attaining a college degree, the program or school should not simply call the nearest university. Instead, they can provide contact information for various colleges, help the individual understand the information, ensure they have support in navigating the college system and connect them with other parents who may have themselves recently gone through a similar process. When considering how to structure parent events and activities, programs and schools may also want to think about (1) providing education and resources that match with goals the parents have identified; (2) identifying different ways to share information using a diverse range of communication methods; (3) providing opportunities for parents to be heard and listened to, whether at meetings with important community or school figures or through one-on-one conversations; and (4) celebrating the smaller successes achieved in the face of multiple challenges, such as opportunities to recognize parents attending their first parent meetings.

●●●

Opportunities for Reflection from the Field

Families whose children attend a school-based Head Start program in their neighborhood would like to ensure that their children have a safe place to play after school. The school playground is within walking distance to many of these families' homes, but the local school board has a strict policy that the playground must be locked up once school is closed. How can the principal of that school help the families organize in order to put a request before the school board to allow children to play in the playground after school?

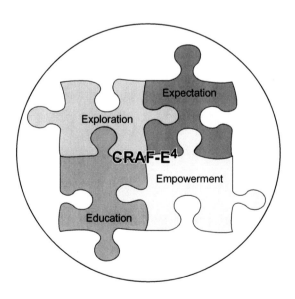

Culturally-Responsive, Anti-bias Framework of Expectation, Education, Exploration, and Empowerment for Family Engagement.

1.3 USING THE CRAF-E^4 TO ENHANCE FAMILY ENGAGEMENT

Numerous studies and reports point to the critical role of families in the success and achievement of young children (Brooks-Gunn & Markman, 2005; Joe & Davis, 2009). This has resulted in the resurgence of work focused on how best to support families, especially racial and ethnic minority families, to be engaged in their child's learning and education. Research has provided evidence about the universal aspects of parenting that is critical for *all* children's success, including minority children. The universal aspects of parenting that have been found to be beneficial for all children regardless of race, ethnicity, and income include sensitive and nurturing parenting and provisions for an enriching environment. In essence, when parents are responsive and sensitive to children's needs and provide a variety of enriching opportunities (e.g., reading and talking, going to plays, and visiting museums), then children's sense of autonomy and confidence in their skills and abilities are enhanced, strengthening their ability to deal with novel stimuli (e.g., learning to read) and overcome obstacles (e.g., insensitive teachers) (Pungello, Iruka, Dotterer, Mills-Koonce, & Reznick, 2009).

However, the challenge is in how best to train practitioners who work and interact with families to incorporate them in a way that is culturally meaningful and sensitive to the context of their daily lives. Rather than viewing minority families as unsupportive, deficient, or uncaring, it is critical for practitioners to continue seeking ways to be more effective in supporting and engaging minority families by becoming more culturally competent.

CHAPTER 2

The Diversity of Families and Changing Demographic Trends

Vignette

Susan is a 2nd grade teacher in an urban school district in Boston. Her students come from diverse racial backgrounds and family structures that are quite different from her upbringing in rural Mississippi where she lived with her mom, dad, and two older brothers. Yet, Susan welcomes the diversity, and she is constantly looking for ways to get to know the families better and to incorporate her students' experiences into class. One of her favorite students is an interracial girl named Meeka whose parents are a lesbian married couple. What are some ways she can incorporate this student's racial diversity into class? What are some strategies Susan can use to connect with Meeka's parents?

The diversity in Susan's class shows the growing change in the United States, especially in regard to families with preschool and school-age children. These demographic changes have implications for the ways that schools and early childhood programs communicate and partner with families to support students' achievement and success. The traditional, one-size-fits-all, way of engaging with families will not be successful. This means that those working with families need to explore the traditions and customs that diverse families bring to their parenting and interactions with practitioners and educators.

2.1 THE CHANGING FACE OF U.S. FAMILIES

How is the face of America changing? The demographics of the United States are changing drastically, especially among young children (those ages 0–8). It has been estimated that racial and ethnic minorities (e.g., Hispanics, Blacks, and Asians) will make up the majority of the population by 2050. As shown in Figure 2.1, the Hispanic percentage of the population will nearly double between 2010 and 2050, and the Asian population will increase as well. The Black population will remain stable, but the White population will decline significantly.

The CRAF-E⁴ Family Engagement Model. DOI: http://dx.doi.org/10.1016/B978-0-12-410415-0.00002-6

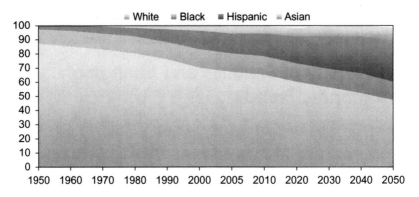

Figure 2.1 Change in major U.S. ethnic groups—1950–2050. Pew Research Center.

These population changes mean teachers will be educating a more racially and ethnically diverse student body in the coming years. Practitioners must understand the strengths and challenges of these families in order to forge meaningful relationships and to foster family engagement.

In addition to the racial and ethnic changes in the population, there are also social changes happening within society. For instance, there are changes in the **poverty level**, **family structure**, and **immigration status** of U.S. families. Even though these social changes affect Whites as well as ethnic and racial minorities, the minorities are often disproportionately affected by these social changes because of their rising numbers in the overall population.

2.1.1 Poverty

In terms of poverty level, as shown in Figure 2.2, although the *percentage* of people living in poverty has decreased since 1959, the total *number* of people in poverty has increased from 1959 until the present time. The increase is from approximately 40 million to 46.5 million (DeNavas-Walt, Proctor, & Smith, 2013).

Although the national average poverty rate was 15%, there were differences across racial and ethnic groups, age groups, gender, and nativity status. These differences indicated that on average Black and Hispanics were more likely to live in poverty than other groups: Over 25% of both African-Americans and Hispanics lived in poverty compared to less than 11% of Whites and 11% of Asians. Children were more likely to live in poverty than adults: Over 20% of individuals under the age of 18 lived in poverty compared to 9% of those over

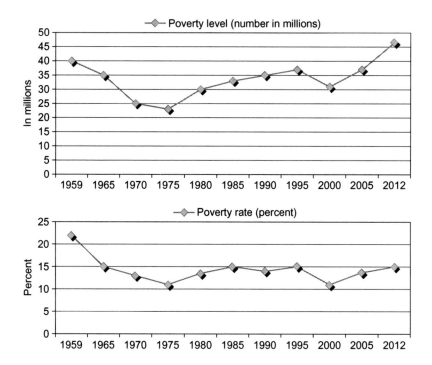

Figure 2.2 Trends in the number and percentage in poverty. DeNavas-Walt, Proctor, and Smith (2013).

65 years old and 14% of those aged 18−64. Women were more likely to live in poverty compared to men (16% vs. 14%). Finally, immigrants were likely to live in poverty compared to native-born individuals (19% vs. 14%).

Teachers and school practitioners need to understand the environmental stressors living in poverty can cause. Such stressors include physical and mental health challenges, food insecurity, poor housing conditions, and low-wage employment (McLoyd, 1990). Chapter 3 discusses these challenges in more detail. There is a need for more contemporary approaches to engaging and partnering with diverse families due to the stressors associated with being poor.

2.1.2 Family Structure
There has been a shift in recent decades regarding many aspects of the family structure in the United States. These shifts included a rise in women being the primary breadwinner, an increase in single parenthood, and a rise in the number of same-sex headed families. These varying family structures indicate that the 1950s iconic *"nuclear*

family" (which included a married man and women with children and the father as the primary breadwinner) has been replaced by a "modern notion of family" that includes individuals who are emotionally bonded yet who may, or may not, be connected biologically or even through a legal status like marriage.

2.1.2.1 "Breadwinner Moms"

Based on the Pew Research Center, in the 1960s, only 11% of mothers were the sole or primary breadwinner in their households, referred to as "**breadwinner moms**" (Parker & Wang, 2013). In 2011, however, over 40% of mothers were breadwinner moms. The rise in these maternal wage earners challenges the notion that a father must be the financial provider for the household. There has been a rise in both single and married women considered to be breadwinner moms: 25% of breadwinner moms were single-mothers and 15% were married-mothers. There is a difference between single and married-mothers though in terms of how much they earn. Parker and Wang (2013) found that over 60% of single-mothers made less than $30,000 per year compared to married-mothers who made $50,000 or more per year. Even more so, single-mother households were more likely to be in poverty compared to married-mother households (6%).

2.1.2.2 Single Parenthood

There has been an increase in single-mothers over the past half a century (Figure 2.3). The reasons for single-motherhood are varied,

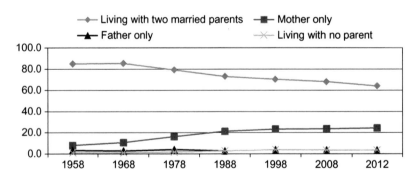

Figure 2.3 Living arrangements of children under 18 years of age from 1970 to 2012.
Note: *Children living with two married parents may be living with biological, adoptive, or nonbiological parents. Children living with mother only or father only may also be living with the parents' unmarried parent.* (www.childtrendsdatabank.org) Data for 2008–2012: Child Trends calculations of U.S. Census Bureau, Current Population Survey, Annual Social and Economic Supplement. "America's Families and Living Arrangements." Tables C-2 and C-3. Available at http://www.census.gov/population/www/socdemo/hh-fam/.html.

including being divorced, widowed, separated, or never married. Despite all the reasons for single-motherhood, those single-mothers that have never married face the most stressors. For example, they tend to be younger (i.e., 30 years old or younger), be of ethnic minority status (i.e., African-American or Hispanic), and nearly half (49%) obtained only a high school education or less. These changes in family structure are also evident by a slight rise in single-father households. (Because men are less likely to live in poverty overall, there are only 16% of single-father households living in poverty). Research shows that a healthy, emotionally functional two-parent family is ideal for a children's well-being primarily because this family type provides financial stability and social and emotional resources (Iruka, 2009; McLanahan, 1983). However, other studies have identified the resiliency of these various other family structures if that the family has adequate resources and is not facing financial hardship.

Figure 2.4 illustrates there are racial and ethnic differences in family structure. Over a quarter of Hispanic children and nearly half of Black children live in single-mother households. In addition, over 6% of Black children live in a household without a parent, which is double the rate for other racial and ethnic groups. Thus, racial and ethnic differences suggest that teachers may need to approach family engagement and even communication with these families differently. For instance, the children living in households without a parent may be living in a *kinship network*, such as with grandparents or other family members. Therefore, extra attempts must be made to ensure that members from these kinship networks feel comfortable engaging in school activities

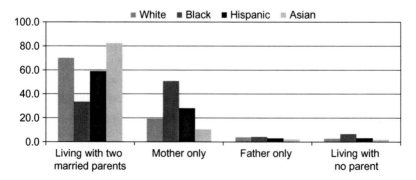

Figure 2.4 Living arrangements of children, by Race and Hispanic Origin, 2012. www.childtrendsdatabank.org Child Trends calculations of U.S. Census Bureau, Current Population Survey, 2012. "America's Families and Living Arrangements: 2012". Table C-2. Available at http://www.census.gov/hhes/families/data/cps2012/html.

and functions. In terms of communication, this means that practitioners must be open to communicating with various types of "caregivers" such as a grandmother, a nonrelative, and a father, and this communication shift inherently requires that a practitioner's ideas about parenthood be expanded to include such "other" types of caregivers.

2.1.2.3 Same-Sex Parents
Recent data show that same-sex couples are raising over 2 million children (Movement Advancement Project, 2011). These families are diverse racially, ethnically, and in terms of their nativity. However, one thing they have in common is that lesbian couples raising families face more financial hardships than heterosexual couples; gay couples do not face such financial hardships. Researchers speculate as to why this may be the case; some argue that the high poverty rate and financial hardships among lesbian parents may be due to gender discrepancy in pay between men and women, employment discrimination due to their sexuality, and/or other stressors associated with being a marginalized family. Researchers have found that children from same-sex families have similar levels of psychological functioning, if not better, than those raised in heterosexual families (Golombok et al., 2003; Movement Advancement Project, 2011). In fact, some studies show children from same-sex families are academically outperforming children from heterosexual families (Gartrell & Bos, 2010).

2.1.3 Immigration
One of the biggest shifts in demographics has been immigration, both authorized and unauthorized. By 2050, racial and ethnic minorities will form the majority of the United States, which is mainly due to the growth in minority children, especially immigrants. This country was built on both voluntary and involuntary (i.e., enslavement) immigration (Ewing, 2012). Figure 2.5 shows the immigration patterns in the past 40 years and the country/region from where most people emigrate. While the vast majority of current immigrants are from Mexico or Latin America (e.g., Central and South America), there are increasing immigrants coming from Africa, Europe, Middle East, and South East Asia (Camarota, 2012).

In addition to the racial and ethnic diversity of the immigrant population, there is diversity in their language ability. Many immigrants are multilingual (Camarota, 2012). Immigrants also vary in their level of English proficiency (i.e., how well they can speak and/or write English). Immigrants from English-speaking countries, such as the United Kingdom,

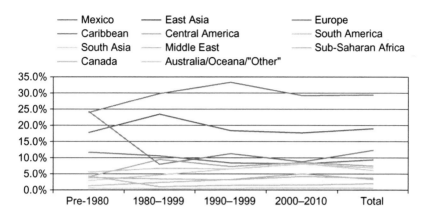

Figure 2.5 Percent of immigrants by region from 1980 to 2010. Camarota, 2012.

or Caribbean countries, such as Trinidad or Jamaica, are fluent in English. This is in contrast to Spanish-speaking countries, such as Mexico and Guatemala, where 50% of individuals from these countries report not being proficient in English. However, the longer immigrants live in the United States, the more their English proficiency increases (Camarota, 2012). Thus, when working with families, it is important to determine their English language proficiency, which is often dependent on their length of time in the United States and their social networks or work environment.

2.2 IMPLICATIONS FOR PRACTICE

2.2.1 Expanding the Meaning of Family Engagement

Traditionally, schools and early education programs define **family engagement** as how much a "parent" is involved in their child's school-based activities (Epstein & Dauber, 1991), such as attending open houses or parent–teacher conferences, volunteering at school, or participating in the Parent–Teacher Organization/Association (PTO/PTA). However, many racial and ethnic minority families who live in poverty do not engage with the school in these expected school-based activities (McWayne, Hampton, Fantuzzo, Cohen, & Sekino, 2004; Mendez, 2010). This is not due to lack of caring for their child's schooling, but for other reasons, including time and availability, transportation problems, or feeling uncomfortable dealing with teachers and other school personnel (Hill, 2001; Parker, Boak, Griffin, Ripple, & Peay, 1999).

The relationship between teachers and parents is often the most critical aspect of family engagement; therefore, strengthening the home–school partnership is crucial for the learning and success of students, especially students of color.

The changing diversity of the United States behooves that practices and norms deemed as *standard* family engagement need to be reevaluated in light of the diverse customs and expectations that minority families may hold. We are not implying that all minority families are unable to be engaged in the traditional way, rather we are arguing that what constitutes family engagement should be expanded so that even those families who cannot engage in traditional ways can be included. For example, parents that live in poverty may not prioritize attending an evening school *Open House* over the opportunity to work an evening shift at their job. However, these parents may be willing to participate in events like inviting parents to have breakfast at school with their children or lunch. Another example is that immigrant parents may believe that their role is to respect the "authority" of school personnel and therefore not interfere or challenge what the school is doing. However, these same families may be open to coming into school to share food or activities that are characteristic of their country of origin. Likewise, a same-sex couple may worry that the school may hold their family in disdain and discriminate against them if they become involved. Teachers can help to eliminate some of this fear by ensuring that the books and pictures around their classroom depict all types of family structures.

There is much heterogeneity in the student population (and their families) in contrast to the homogeneity of the teaching personnel in K–12 (i.e., mostly White, middle-class women) (Aud, Fox, & KewalRamani, 2010). Teachers in the early childhood age groups are more diverse. For instance, the T.E.A.C.H. Early Childhood scholarship program reports that 48% of the recipients of their scholarship program were people of color (Child Care Services Association, 2013). School practitioners should discover how best to engage, interact, and partner with families who may or may not be different from themselves. So, what preliminary actions should teachers and practitioners take in strengthening family engagement with families of color, same-sex couple families, and/or non-English-speaking families?

2.2.2 Explore Diversity! Suggestions for Activities and Strategies for Building Relationships with Families

• Learn more about the level of diversity of students and families in the center, school, or program. For example, find out the percent of families with one non-English-speaking member, percent of families living in poverty, or the different types of family structures.

- Find out about families' cultural customs and values through home visits and conversations with parents (e.g., children roles in the home or the child's relationship with the extended family). In addition, teachers should try to find out what the families' traditions and country of origin are? What things do families do during the weekend?
- Take stock of school practices that may deter parents from engaging. For example, are meeting locations accessible by public transportation or are meeting times restricted to certain times of day? Revise communication strategies that may not reflect diversity (e.g., do forms assume a nuclear family structure? Are materials only in English?)

Opportunities for Reflection from the Field

One school system in the southeast decided to find out how diverse families engage in their children's learning, by conducting focus groups (Gillanders, Iruka, Ritchie, & Cobb, 2013). These focus groups were structured so that families from similar backgrounds participated in the same group (e.g., Latina mothers, White dads) and so that a professional from the same ethnic group facilitated it (e.g., a Latina practitioner facilitated the focus group with Latina mothers). Keeping the groups similar allowed the parents to feel safe and understood, and this is a recommended practice when conducting focus groups. Parents were asked questions ranging from their goals for their child and their beliefs about their role in their child's education and learning how they wanted to be involved with the school and their child's learning. For example, parents reported that they had the highest expectation for their child, wanted to be involved, and were often engaging their child in academic activities at home. However, they were not confident in being part of the school system or did not have a way to better connect with teachers and other parents. This type of information and others was summarized and presented to the school system with potential recommendations to revise practices and policies to better meet the needs of their diverse population.

2.3 REFLECTION QUESTIONS FOR TEACHERS AND PRACTITIONERS

1. Do you have friends or family from different racial or ethnic backgrounds? How does the diversity enhance your perspectives?

2. Do you think the changing family structures pose a problem for children's school success? Why or why not? What can you do to build bridges with these families in order to help foster children's school success?
3. What does the trend in immigration mean for how you connect with families whose native language is not English?

CHAPTER 3

Providing Resources to Help Address Challenges Faced by Families

Vignette

Roxanne is a family worker employed in a northeastern urban Head Start program. Natasha Fidalgo is one of the students on Roxanne's case load. Natasha and her family are from Cape Verde, an island off the coast of Africa where the dominant language is Portuguese. Her family recently came to the United States to visit and then decided to stay because her father got a job as an engineer at a manufacturing company. Though Natasha's family is educated and speaks some English, her parents do not want to have home visits. Though Roxanne tried different ways to get the families to come meet with her at school, Natasha's parents never respond to her queries. How can Roxanne engage this family?

3.1 BECOMING EDUCATED ABOUT THE CHALLENGES

Regardless of their nationality, language, race/ethnicity, religion, sexual orientation, or disability status, families all over the world face challenges in trying to meet the needs of their children. For minority families, these challenges are often compounded by discrimination, social isolation, and economic deprivation.

As discussed in Chapter 1, minority families and immigrant families are more likely to live in poverty compared to White and native-born families (Costello, Keeler, & Angold, 2001; U.S. Department of Education, 2007). Poverty is associated with lower educational attainment, higher unemployment, poor health, and psychological stressors. Living in poverty affects daily life choices, such as the house one can buy or rent, the community resources people have access to, and the schools children will attend.

The CRAF-E⁴ Family Engagement Model. DOI: http://dx.doi.org/10.1016/B978-0-12-410415-0.00003-8

3.1.1 Education Challenges

While there has been a positive trend of Blacks and Latinos attaining a high school diploma and college degree, this percentage is still behind the average for Whites (Figure 3.1). For example, while the percentage of White females with a college degree increased from 18% to over 40% between 1973 and 2009, the increase of Black females during this same time period is 8−21% and of Latinas 3%−15%. Policy changes such as Title IX are thought to have played an instrumental role in providing access for women to attend college, particularly via the use of college sports (Han, 2007; U.S. Department of Justice, 2012).

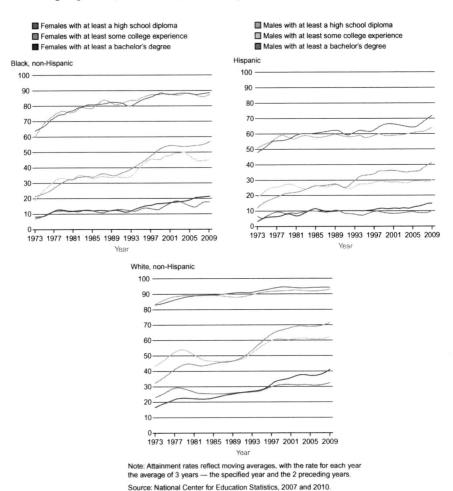

Note: Attainment rates reflect moving averages, with the rate for each year the average of 3 years — the specified year and the 2 preceding years.

Source: National Center for Education Statistics, 2007 and 2010.

Figure 3.1 Percentage of individuals aged 25−29 who have completed high school, some college or a bachelor's degree, by race/ethnicity and gender, 1973−2009. http://trends.collegeboard.org/education-pays/figures-tables/ educational-attainment-race-ethnicity-and-gender-1973-2009.

3.1.2 Employment Challenges

African-Americans are twice as likely to be unemployed than Whites, and even those who are employed suffer from wage discrimination. Wage discrimination is the discrepancy in the average wages between two more more groups. For instance, on average, African-American men earn 72 cents compared to the dollar that the White men earn; also, an African-American man only earns 85 cents on the dollar compared to White women (Rodgers, 2008). This sort of wage discrimination will impact the kind of life an African-American man will be able to provide for his family. As given in Table 3.1, the employment and unemployment rate and the earnings vary between Blacks, Hispanics, and Whites. Even when Blacks have college degrees, they are almost twice as likely to be unemployed compared to their White counterparts (Figure 3.2).

Table 3.1 Unemployment, Employment, and Earnings Characteristics by Race and Hispanic Ethnicity[a], 2011 Annual Averages			
Characteristics of the Employed	Blacks	Whites	Hispanics
% Employed (employment-population ratio among those 16 and older)	51.7	59.4	58.9
% Usually working part time	18.0	19.9	18.9
% Women (age 16 and older)	53.8	46.0	40.6
% College graduates (age 25 and older)	26.5	36.8	16.7
% Working in the private sector (wage and salary workers)	76.9	78.5	83.7
% Working in the public sector	19.3	14.2	10.4
% Self-employed (unincorporated)[b]	3.8	7.2	5.8
Usual Median Weekly Earnings			
Total ($)	615	775	549
Men ($)	653	856	571
Women ($)	595	703	518
Characteristics of the Unemployed			
Unemployment rate	15.8	7.9	11.5
% Women (age 16 and older)	46.9	43.0	41.9
Median duration of unemployment in weeks	27.0	19.7	18.5
% Long-term unemployed (27 weeks or more)	49.5	41.7	39.9

[a] *Persons whose ethnicity is identified as Hispanic or Latino may be of any race. Those identified as White or Black include those Hispanics who selected White or Black when queried about their race.*
[b] *Self-employed refers to self-employed workers whose businesses are unincorporated.*
Source: *Bureau of Labor Statistics, Current Population Survey.*

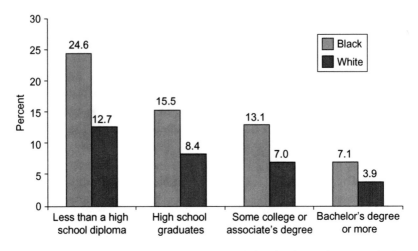

Figure 3.2 Unemployment rate for Blacks and Whites aged 25 and older, by educational attainment, 2011 annual average. Bureau of Labor Statistics, Current Population Survey.

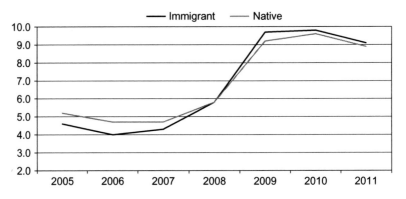

Figure 3.3 Unemployment rate for natives and immigrants, 2005–2011. Bureau of Labor Statistics from the Current Population Survey. http://cnsnews.com/news/article/bls-unemployment-higher-among-native-born-immigrants.

On the other hand, the employment rate for immigrants was slightly higher than for natives (Figure 3.3). However, there has been a recent surge in unemployment among immigrants. For instance, unemployment was especially evident for those with less education, but even educated immigrants saw an increase in their unemployment rate compared to natives, an increase of 3.7% for immigrants versus 1.5% for natives (Camarota & Jensenius, 2009). While the unemployment rate for immigrants with the least education was explained because they were likely to have jobs harder hit by the recession, it is unclear why educated immigrants saw a steep increase in their unemployment rate compared to natives.

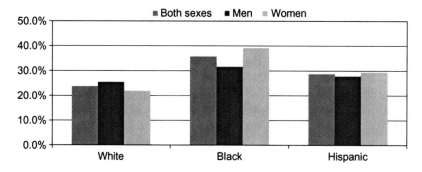

Figure 3.4 Obesity among adults by race/ethnicity and sex, 2006–2008. Centers for Disease Control and Prevention. http://www.cdc.gov/Features/dsObesityAdults/.

3.1.3 Physical Health Challenges

Diverse families who live in poverty are also likely to have less access to health care which results in them having untreated illnesses or procedures and/or hospitalizations for illnesses that could have been avoided had they had access to preventative health care (Fiscella, Franks, Gold, & Clancy, 2000). Black and Hispanic children are less likely to have a primary care provider compared to White children, which is critical for receiving adequate preventative care (30% and 20% vs. 16%) (http://www.ahrq.gov/research/findings/factsheets/minority/disparit/). Additionally, Blacks and Hispanics are likely to rely on clinics and emergency rooms for medical care compared to Whites (http://www.ahrq.gov/research/findings/factsheets/minority/disparit/).

Some of the health risks facing low-income infants are being born low-birth weight (i.e., less than 5 1/2 pounds) and increased chances of dying during the first year of life (infant mortality). (Currie, 2005; Mays, Cochran, & Barnes, 2006). Other studies have shown that the rate of obesity is increasing among young Black and Latina girls (Wang & Beydoun, 2007), and this disparity begins prenatally and during early childhood (Taveras et al., 2010). According to the Centers for Disease Control and Prevention (CDC), Blacks are more likely to be obese, followed by Hispanics and then Whites (Figure 3.4).

3.1.4 Mental Health Challenges

In addition to the psychological stressor of being a minority, being poor and a minority has been associated with increased odds of being diagnosed with schizophrenia (Chow et al., 2003). Furthermore, Blacks are at higher risk for involuntary psychiatric commitment than any other racial group with poor Blacks and Latinos more likely to be referred for commitment by a law enforcement official than any other racial group (Chow et al., 2003). There have been mixed findings about the rates of depression across ethnic groups. Studies have suggested that Whites are likely to *report* higher rates of major depression[1] compared to Blacks and Latinos, but Whites are less likely to report chronic depression, depression lasting two or more years.[2] Chronic depression is higher among Blacks and Latinos. The reason why chronic depression may be lower for Whites is due to access to adequate treatment, including psychotropic drugs and positive beliefs about seeking mental health care (Riolo et al., 2005). An often overlooked contributor to depression is racism. Numerous studies link racism to depression. For instance, in one study, African-Americans who held doctoral degrees or who were pursuing a doctorate degree reported incidences of racial discrimination during 26% of the total study days, such as being ignored, denied service, or overlooked (Ong et al., 2009). These perceived discriminatory incidences were associated with higher levels of negative effect, anxiety, and depression. Similarly, another study showed that Latino immigrants who perceived they were targets of racism were showing high rates of sleep disturbances, which are precursors to depression (Steffen & Bowden, 2006).

3.2 IMPLICATIONS FOR PRACTICE

Minority families experience more stressors that are likely confounded with poverty than are nonminorities. For practitioners who are working with minority families, they should be aware of the life circumstances of these families, especially families living and raising a child in poverty. While all families have assets and strengths that are crucial for the optimal development of their child (which we will discuss further in Chapter 4), financial challenges can have a particular impact on parents' ability to meet the material needs of their child.

---

[1]According to the National Institute of Mental Health, major depressive disorder is characterized by a combination of symptoms that interfere with a person's ability to work, sleep, study, eat, and enjoy once-pleasurable activities (http://www.nimh.nih.gov/health/publications/depression/index.shtml).
[2]Chronic depression, or dysthymia, is characterized by a long-term (2 years or more) depressed mood. There are also symptoms present that are associated with major depression but not enough for a diagnosis of major depression. Chronic depression is less severe than major depression and typically does not disable the person.

●●●————————————————————————————————

Opportunities for Reflection from the Field

Consider the parent who has been unemployed for over nine months whose unemployment insurance is about to run out. She has been looking for work every day, but she has yet to get an interview. Though she gets out of bed to make sure her three children get to the bus stop for school, she is feeling quite anxious because she is unsure if she will have enough money to pay her car note or buy gas to go grocery shopping. When you call to talk to her about her daughter needing some educational services, she does not return your calls.

————————————————————————————————

Research has found that when parents have economic pressure, they are likely to exhibit depressive symptoms, which can impact their engagement with their child's learning and development (Conger et al., 1992; Conger et al., 1994). What this means is that practitioners need to support parents in minimizing their economic pressure through providing resources and networks to assist them. This may mean practitioners helping parents find their neighborhood job search centers, informing them of resources that may be available in the community, and connecting them with public assistance networks and social support.

In many instances, practitioners are aware of families going through challenges. This may be an impetus for practitioners to be more active in soliciting information and services from local community agencies and organizations. Although families may live in a community for many years, they may not be aware of all the resources available in their community. Especially for immigrant families, practitioners can serve as resource brokers by connecting families to good services and information, such as nutrition, health care, child care, housing, and educational services. In addition to services that directly benefit the child, one can also help families find services to support them, including job training, language classes, and drug abuse counseling.

3.2.1 Educate Yourself About Challenges! Suggestions and Strategies for Practice

What are the critical steps to supporting families who face challenges?

- Educate and provide information and resources to families
- Find out about the families' needs (without judgment)
- Find out about the families' source of support and networks

- Find out about available resources and information in the community
- Connect families with available resources and support
- Follow up with families about their use of the recommended resources
- Follow up with the agency about any new services they or others are providing that may be beneficial for families you serve

Beyond economic pressure, other challenges to family engagement include practitioner's biases and negative stereotypes that parents, especially low-income and minority families' do not want to be engaged, disconnect with children's home culture, parents' limited English proficiency, and logistical issues, such as work schedule, transportation, and child care (Curenton & Iruka, 2013). In response to these challenges, practitioners can do the following to support families:

- Seek ways to ensure that parents are viewed as critical decision makers
- Provide communication in parents' home language
- Provide information that is simple and clear to the layperson
- Recognize the value of the parents' home culture
- Ensure that meeting times and location are convenient for the parent (Curenton & Iruka, 2013).

3.3 REFLECTION QUESTIONS

1. What are the biggest challenges of the families you work with and how can you equip them to handle them?
2. What is a resource you can offer a mother who is unemployed and seeking assistance to cover her child's afterschool care while she looks for work?
3. What do you see as some of the reasons for these racial and ethnicity disparities in poverty and stressful life circumstances (e.g., society, education, families themselves)?
4. How do the life challenges between non-English-speaking immigrants differ from English-speaking immigrants?

CHAPTER 4

Understanding the Strengths and Resilience of Diverse Families

Vignette

Jackie is an African-American 30-year-old single-mother working at Walmart. She is the mother of twin preschool boys. The family became homeless two months ago when Jackie got behind on the rent due to the mounting medical bills for the youngest twin who has autism. Being homeless upsets their nighttime routine because they are staying at the home of different church members each night. As a result, the twins are often tired and hungry when they arrive to school in the morning. Jackie's church members have been instrumental in helping her navigate this difficulty. Despite these challenges, Jackie remains optimistic because of her strong religious faith, and she remains active in attending her weekly church services.

4.1 BUILDING ON THE STRENGTHS AND RESILIENCY OF DIVERSE FAMILIES

Racial and ethnic minorities represent a diversity of cultures and traditions that have strengths and resiliency that are often not acknowledged or utilized to support families and their children. **Resiliency** is defined as the ability to thrive despite facing harsh conditions. The research literature contains many examples of how racial and ethnic minority families are resilient. For example, there is a rich history of a close-knit extended family, religiosity/spirituality, community values of collectivism, perseverance through discrimination, flexible use of language, innovation and exemplary artistic expression, and athletic prowess. These cultural practices that show resilience need to be identified and integrated into the experiences of young children, as well as used as resources in bringing and integrating new information into children's learning. These practices form the social fabric that dictates norms and social mores in most racial and ethnic minority families and helps them to be resilient in the face of social and structural obstacles.

The CRAF-E⁴ Family Engagement Model. DOI: http://dx.doi.org/10.1016/B978-0-12-410415-0.00004-X

4.1.1 Close-Knit Extended Families

One of the greatest strengths of racial and ethnic minority families is their strong supportive ties to extended kinship networks, or extended kin. Extended families, or kinship networks, is the bedrock of many minority families, especially those who have recently immigrated.

In many minority cultures, the entire community is viewed as being responsible for the rearing of a child. Hence, the African proverb, "It takes a village to raise a child." This is truly the case in many native born and immigrant Black families. It is not uncommon to see several members of a family living in the same space. These family members care for the well-being of all the children. Instead of assuming that the family is poor because they are "crowded," one must understand the rationale of how this "crowded" living is viewed from the perspective of the family members. In that, one's family is there to protect and support them, so it is viewed as a benefit rather than a burden. The extended family system offers checks and balances and helps in raising children, along with minimizing the economic and emotional pressure of raising a child.

The extended family serves multiple purposes, and this kinship networks provide both emotional support and instrumental support. Examples of emotional support include talking with someone about your problems or feelings, seeking advice, and just spending leisure time with people in your family network. Extended family members provide the sense of belonging and connection and thus limit the sense of isolation that some immigrant families feel (Spencer & Markstrom-Adams, 1990). Examples of instrumental support include helping people with concrete resources they need to survive, such as lending money, providing housing, baby sitting, or giving car rides. The use of extended family for child care is quite evident in the Latino community where young children are often not in formal center-based care but in relative home-based care (Sarkisian et al., 2006; Uttal, 1999). In the case of immigrants, many emigrate to a community where they have extended family and ethnic networks to support their acculturation into the United States.

4.1.1.1 The Role of Grandparents

Grandparents often play a special role in the extended family. Grandparents, are often called to serve as primary caregivers in certain situations when the parents are having difficulty, including illness or disability, divorce, teen pregnancy, parent abuse or neglect, single parent

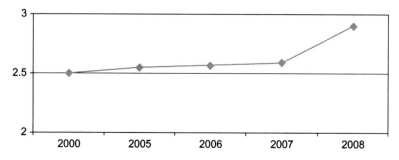

Figure 4.1 Sharp increase in children with grandparent caregivers since 2007. Pew Research Center Calculations of Decennial Census and American Community Survey Data.

parenthood, drug and alcohol abuse, and incarceration (Livingston & Parker, 2010). Recent statistics show an uptack in grandparents being primary caregivers beginning in 2007, during the time of the Great Recession (Figure 4.1). Though traditionally African-American and Hispanic children were more likely to be raised by their grandparents, during the Great Recession, there was an increase of 9% in White children being raised by their grandparents compared to 2% of African-Americans and no change for Hispanics. However, African-American children were more likely to live in a household where they have been formally placed with their grandparents as their primary caregiver (Harden et al., 1997; U.S. Census/C2SS, 2001). In addition to economic reasons, grandparent care is also due to the Black culture of grand parents being seeing as critical and stable forces in helping raise children (Burton & Dilworth-Anderson, 1991).

4.1.1.2 The Role of Elders
One such example of tradition that is often stressed in some diverse families (e.g., Africans and Asians) is the reverence held for the elders. Elders are defined as adults in late adulthood (age 65 or older) who are viewed as having life experiences and wisdom that enables them to give advice to those in younger generations. The elders are viewed as the individuals who guide the family to the "righteous" path by pointing out what is "proper" or "disgraceful" behaviors in their culture. The elders are particularly critical in helping the younger generation understand that their behaviors are a reflection on the family, community, and culture. Furthermore, in some diverse families, the value of honor is very important (Fuligni et al., 1999). To these communities, honor is defined

as respecting the authority, wishes, and expectation of the family. For example, children are expected to forego their own desires for the benefit of the family and community, as in the instance where children are encouraged to take a prestigious job (e.g., engineering, medicine) rather than one that is viewed as more fanciful (e.g., artist, chef).

4.1.2 Religiosity and Spirituality

Religiosity and/or spirituality play a prominent role in the lives of many minority families. Research has pointed to the protective factor of religion in the lives of racial and ethnic minority families, especially African-Americans in the face of discrimination, prejudice, and even violence during the enslavement and Jim Crows era (Bierman, 2006; Gary, 1995; Jeynes, 2003). Being reared in a religious family serves as a protector factor for children because children are less likely to engage in delinquent activity or become pregnant during adolescence, and they are more likely to get good grades. Most members of the minority populations have their own beliefs such as religious and spiritual practices that are cultural and indigenous. Among these groups are Christians, Muslims, animists, pagans, and atheists. These religious practices may impact how families function and subsequently their interaction with schools and school personnel. For example, certain religions (e.g., Muslim) do not allow married women to be in the presence of another male who is not a relative, or the religion may have expectations that matters concerning children that may only be discussed with the father or male family members. In other instances, some students may not come to school on Fridays due to their religion. In addition, some Seven-day Adventists students and families are unable to participate in afterschool activities on Friday evenings and Saturdays due to Sabbath activities. These examples emphasize the importance of practitioners understanding how religious beliefs and practices can impact their interactions and partnerships with families.

4.1.3 Cultural Socialization

Even universal models of parenting are characterized by cultural models of parenting that include the goals, ideology, values, and beliefs of the parents within a particular cultural group, referred to as **cultural socialization**. For racial and ethnic minorities, this cultural socialization, also referred to as racial socialization, includes multiple dimensions, specially, (a) teaching children about their heritage, (b) preparing them for bias and discrimination, (c) and teaching them about the commonalities (and sometimes differences) among other ethnic groups (Hughes, 2003; Hughes and Chen, 1997, 1999; McAdoo, 2002; Suzzio et al., 2009). Repeated research has shown racial socialization to be a protective factor for African American children. Children whose parents report using such socialization techniques have children who are more successful academically and emotionally healthy (Caughy et al., 2002, 2004). Extended family plays a key role in this cultural socialization, specifically as it relates to teaching about heritage, by sharing family histories and stories and exposing children to culture events and activities. In many instances, elders help protect the religious mores as practiced in their countries of origin, and even church communities play a pivotal role in this cultural socialization. The goal of cultural socialization is to ensure that children do not forget the tradition and values of their culture, to instill a positive sense of cultural identity and pride, and to prepare them for the future discrimination that they might face.

4.1.4 Key Cultural value of "Showing Respect"
In many racial and ethnic minority cultures, "showing respect" is the fundamental cultural value. In Mexican culture, this cultural value is referred to as *respectivo*. Respect is often shown through both language and nonverbal communication. For example, respect can be shown by properly greeting people and referring to them using the correct name or salutation (e.g., Mister, Madame, Doctor, and Reverend). For instance, in some African cultures, the idea of calling a married woman by her first name is a sign of disrespect. Respect can also be shown by a bow, such as the *mano po* in the Filipino culture, or understanding that it is _not_ customary to initiate any physical contact with certain families members, such as the Muslim tradition of no cross-gender physical touch with people outside the family. Respect is also show by allowing people to *save face*, that is not embarrassing or insulting people. It is extremely important in racial and ethnic minority cultures that respect is shown to elders, and it is also important that parents (or family members) or not "disrespected" in front of their children.

Another manner of showing respect is through valuing minority families' traditions and culture by incorporating their traditions and culture in all aspects of the program, school, or classroom. This means going beyond displaying pictures or artifacts, but also seeing different cultures as adding value to those in the program, school, and classroom. For example, this may mean inviting parents from diverse backgrounds to participate in the development of activities, events, and lessons, in addition to engaging them in any formal decision-making structure, such as PTO/PTA.

4.2 IMPLICATIONS FOR PRACTICE

As practitioners seek to identify and determine ways to engage, interact, and partner with families, they must begin to understand the lives of these families. As many teachers for example live in separate communities than their students, a huge gulf exists because of the disconnection between teachers' and students' lives. So many practitioners are seen as making little or no effort to understand the cultures and lives of the students and their families. They must first show respect and value for families' culture and traditions, and be conscious of how their behavior may be viewed inadvertently viewed as disrespectful. For instance, not verbally greeting a parent when they walk into the classroom can be interpreted as disrespectful. In addition, many practitioners and professionals that work in urban areas are afraid to visit parents or go into the neighborhoods, but refusing to step in someone's house is regarded as an insult.

One way to strengthen the connection with families is to inquire about their lives and cultures. For example, one can ask who makes up the "family." Is the family only a mother and father, father and a grandmother, etc.? What extended family can parents and students call upon? Determining the extended family will help one call on the resources of a student beyond just the primary caregiver. For example, in the instances that the primary caregiver cannot attend a meeting or event, one may be able to include the extended family. These extended family members may also serve as an intermediary to strengthen families' engagement. One must also realize that extended family may include "fictive kin" (meaning people who are not biologically related but who are still considered to be family) whose role should not be minimized because they are not biologically related to the family or student, but rather supported.

The family traditions, including spiritual guidance held by families, may be antithetical to interacting and partnering with practitioners, at least as viewed by many practitioners. However, rather than assumptions being made about how a family's culture may negatively impact family engagement, it is important that practitioners understand how these traditions may actually be viewed from a strength-based perspective. For example, one may assume that a family where the mother is not allowed to meet without her husband may restrict and limit meeting times. However, it can be viewed as positive in that the fathers are assured of being directly included in all aspects of their child's learning rather than indirectly. As many programs often do not effectively include fathers or males, it may require that more attention be given to involving and engaging fathers and males in the family. Thus, practitioners who endeavor to understand the intricacies of the extended families, cultural norms, and religiosity in a culturally sensitive way are more likely to have cooperative partners from these families.

As many diverse parents are often seeking avenues to build cultural pride beyond the home, avenues that practitioners provide to incorporate families' culture would be viewed as a form of respect and in turn may likely lead to stronger home–school relationships. In addition to surrounding children with extended family and exposing them to family traditions, which may also include religious practices and celebrations, practitioners can support minority families' cultural socialization practices through exposing students to positive, diverse, and nonstereotypic images about their culture. Rather than just exposing minority children to entertainers and athletes, stories and images of other professions such as scientists, artists, directors, and engineers should be shown and often incorporated in readings, discussions, and events. Thus, partnership with minority families can support practitioners in being able to authentically incorporate students' culture and tradition in all aspects of the programs, school, and classroom.

4.3 REFLECTION QUESTIONS

1. What are some of the strengths of the minority families you work with?
2. How do your interactions with families show that you value and understand their cultural strengths and resiliencies?
3. How can you systematically incorporate these strengths into the classroom and into your meetings with families?

CHAPTER 5

Examination of Teachers' and Practitioners' Biases

Vignette

After Hurricane Katrina, Becky decided to head to Louisiana to teach 3rd grade. Becky was having a hard time connecting with the children and families in the community, and she could not understand why. Finally, during a one-on-one parent meeting with the grandmother of the smartest student in her class, Becky opened up and asked the grandmother if she had any suggestions for how she could emotionally connect with more families and how she could provide them with educational resources the families might need. The grandmother said, "Well, maybe it would be a good idea for you to hold some parent meetings about how to get them thinking about going to college." "College?" Becky silently thought to herself. It was at that moment that she realized she had never thought about her students attending college in the future. She had been inadvertently operating from the low expectation of just hoping that most of them would graduate from high school.

5.1 ADDRESSING PRACTITIONER BIAS

Biases include **stereotypes**, which are overly simplified generalizations about a group of people who share a common culture, race, nationality, or other characteristic. **Prejudice** is preconceived unfavorable judgments based on stereotypes. These biased thoughts can then lead to **discrimination**, which is the act of favoring or going against an individual due to their membership in a group. While the population of minority students is increasing (Figure 5.1), this same dramatic change in the student population has not been seen with teachers though there is a steady decline in White teachers and increase in teachers of color (Figure 5.2).

The CRAF-E⁴ Family Engagement Model. DOI: http://dx.doi.org/10.1016/B978-0-12-410415-0.00005-1

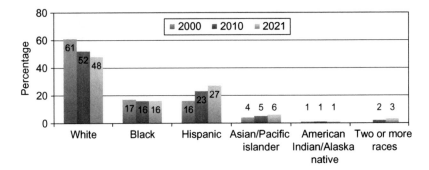

Figure 5.1 Percentage of U.S. public school students enrolled in prekindergarten through 12th grade, by racelethnicity, fall 2000–fall 2021. U.S. Department of Education, National Center for Education Statistics, Projections of Education Statistics to 2021; and Common Core of Data (CCD), "State Nonfiscal Survey of Public Elementary and Secondary Education," selected years, 2000–01 through 2010–11. See Digest of Education Statistics 2012, table 44.

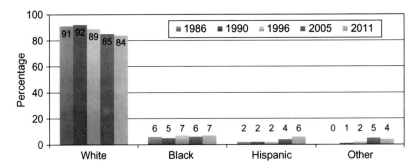

Figure 5.2 Percentage of U.S. public school teachers kindergarten through 12th grade, by racelethnicity, fall 1986–fall 2011.

●●●

Opportunities for Reflection from the Field

During a one-on-one meeting with the director of an early childhood program, an African-American parent, Shelia, voiced the concern that every minority teacher who had been hired over the course of the year quit their jobs at the center, often abruptly and without any clear explanation being given to the parents. Shelia was concerned because her daughter was one of the few Black children enrolled in the center, and she wanted to ensure that her child had at least one teacher who could serve as a role model for her. The director, who was a White woman, assured Shelia that there was no "underlying issue" within the center. She explained that none of the minority staff had ever come to her to complain that they felt uncomfortable in any way, and the director went on to explain how the center collects a yearly survey that asks a question about whether or not the center is welcoming of diversity. When Shelia tried to explain that teachers might actually be afraid to come to the director with issues or to complain on a survey, especially given that these minorities were always positioned as the "lone minority" in the center, the director disagreed and assured Shelia that she fostered a working environment that valued diversity. How is this director's denial and defensiveness demonstrating her bias? Why might an attitude such as this alienate staff and parents?

The vast majority of teaching professionals and many other school practitioners in K–12 public schools are White women. As one's cultural background among other things guides one's thinking and view of the world, it is not surprising that many practitioners judge students and families based on Eurocentric ideals, cultures, and stereotypes. Considering the potential for misinterpreting cultural-based behaviors, cultural competence, or lack thereof is beginning to emerge as one of the main impediments for practitioners being able to establish a strong home–school partnership.

That is, teachers and other practitioners come across students and families who are different from them and most are unable to deal with these families in a way that is culturally sensitive. They often base their assessment of families and students on the stereotypes about that group. For example, teachers may think that a student is lying because the student does not look directly at them. Then in some instances, guilt is automatically assumed rather than considering that certain cultures require that children not look at elders or authority figures when spoken to as a sign of respect. While it is a Eurocentric norm for children to engage in contingent and back-and-forth conversations with adults, in some cultures, this is not encouraged as it shows a sign of disobedience and disrespect.

Starting when children enter kindergarten, teachers, paraprofessionals, and other school staff are unable to effectively build a strong partnership and relationship with minority families and support them to navigate through the educational system and advocate for their child's needs (Boethel, 2003). While many professionals are well intentioned, their biases based on their own cultures and upbringing may impact how they connect with minority families and children. This requires that practitioners are culturally competent. Cross et al. (1989) discuss that being culturally competent is not a one-time event but a learning process that goes through developmental stages. The stages, shown in Figure 5.3, include cultural destructiveness, cultural incapacity, cultural blindness, cultural precompetence, cultural competence, and proficiency.

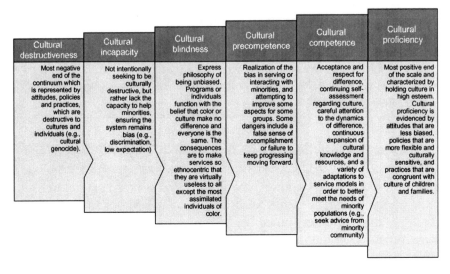

Figure 5.3 Developmental stages to becoming culturally competent.

These developmental stages of cultural competence require that practitioners question their attitudes, as well as their organizations' attitudes toward diverse families. These "attitudes" can come in the form of policies and practices that devalue families' cultures.

In most urban areas where there are large populations of different cultures, the administrative structure of the school systems creates barriers with some policies that are not conducive to engaging with minority students and their families. Policies such as "English only" indicate to non-English-speaking families that their home language, as well as their culture, is not valued or appreciated. This may lead to families not feeling comfortable engaging with school or school personnel, discouraging any potential relationships between families and schools. Barriers that may seem even culturally sensitive, such as the one below may result in negative outcomes.

●●●————————————————————————————————————

Opportunities for Reflection from the Field

In an example from one of the authors (Dr. Winnie Eke), a 10-year veteran high school science teacher in a northeast urban school district, she recounted having a student from Somalia[1] who had never been in a

————————

[1] Different countries used to protect students' identity.

school until he came to her school. This student was placed in her 10th-grade science class based on his age. This proved to be very difficult to the student, parents, and the teacher. First, the student's educational status was not discussed to prepare the teacher. Second, the student was very uncomfortable in the class and had no way of discussing his predicament with Dr. Eke due to the cultural barrier or not wanting to disappoint her (teachers were held in high regard in his African culture). After the first test, Dr. Eke spoke to the student with the help of a translator about his work and discovered the academic deficiencies, including the fact that he did not attend school beyond the 3rd grade because he had to work to help his family. Due to the placement of this student in the 3rd grade without consideration for his prior school experiences and ability, it caused shame and embarrassment to the family due to their son being unable to grasp the lessons and his grades suffering, which resulted in the family not feeling comfortable with engaging with Dr. Eke and other school personnel. Thus, in the attempt to be culturally blind, the school created a barrier to engaging with the family and potentially destroying the students' confidence and joy in learning.

5.2 IMPLICATIONS FOR PRACTICE

As a way to minimize the impact of bias in partnering with minority families for the benefit of their children, one must become more culturally competent. Diller and Moule (2005) point out that in order to become culturally competent, one must develop "certain personal and interpersonal awareness and sensitivities, developing certain bodies of cultural knowledge and mastering a set of skills that, taken together, underlie effective cross-cultural teaching." The skills needed to become cultural proficient include (a) valuing diversity, (b) engaging in self-assessment and self-awareness, (c) assessing the culture of your organization, (d) understanding the history of cultural interactions, (e) institutionalizing cultural knowledge, and (f) adapting to diversity.

Valuing diversity—the foundation to connecting with minority families is to acknowledge and respect families' culture, including their history, traditions, and practices. This would require that one inquires about the traditions and practices and becomes more knowledgeable about how ones' cultural background shapes their perception of the world. For example, one may view African-American parenting practices as harsh and punitive; however, when viewed through the history of enslavement and discrimination and ensuring that children are protected from racial violence, one may understand this approach to parenting as protective.

Engaging in self-assessment and self-awareness—while the majority of this book encourages learning more about families, a critical aspect of partnering and engaging with minority families is for one to understand their own views, biases, and perceptions of the world and others. In their work on strengthening cultural competence of early education teachers, Curenton and Iruka (2013) suggest one way to become self-aware—asking yourself the positive and negative aspects of your cultural group, including the perceived positive and negative aspects and then asking the same questions for other ethnic groups. For example, do you see your group as resilient in the face of discrimination but another group as less resilient? Do you then view individuals from this group as weak and helpless?

Assessing the cultural organizations—schools and school systems are organizations that have been functioning the same way for hundreds of years. Majority White students have been in these schools and systems for those years. This then means that the culture of home–school partnership has been based on these majority families. The culture of the organizations may be in direct opposition to the culture of minority families. Oftentimes schools develop schedules for parent–teacher conferences or meetings with specific beginning and ending time; however, some minority families may not have the same sense of time and so they may not be as rigid in adhering to the time structure. This may then create a tension between families and professionals. Other aspects of the organizations to consider include whether certain groups are often restricted to particular positions (e.g., African-American aide, Hispanic administrative assistant, White principal) or meetings are held in only English regardless of the makeup of the program or school. By inquiring about all aspects of your organizations, one can begin to pinpoint where potential changes can be made to be more culturally sensitive and more inviting to minority families.

Understanding the history of cultural interactions—while the United States is often viewed as multicultural, it is important to note that the United States also has a history of discrimination and oppression. This history continues to covertly impact how members of different cultural groups interact. Being sensitive to racial differences is not an indication of being a racist. Thus, being aware that minority families engage with practitioners of color in a more intimate and informal fashion compared to a White practitioner is an indication of how history impacts interactions across cultural groups. However, awareness of the history of the United States, especially in regard to groups that have a history of oppression and disenfranchisement will allow one to not see these behaviors as negative, but as adaptive and valuable to families of color.

Institutionalizing cultural knowledge—while some may believe that it is easier to be "color-blind," it is a disservice to families and students when one does not acknowledge their experiences, contexts, histories, and traditions. Thus, one way to becoming culturally competent is being able to seamlessly incorporate and consider families' culture into all aspects of the organization's practices and policies. In order to do this, one must become familiar with the different cultures of their families. This can only be done through communication and engagement with families as well as discussions and discoveries with program personnel.

Adapting to diversity—this does not mean to merely eat the food of a cultural group, but rather to find ways to actively seek out and integrate the culture of the family in all aspects of the program. For example, determine if there are key cultural holidays that should appear in the school calendar beyond the U.S. holidays. Is there an assumption that only mothers and fathers are allowed to attend parent–teacher conferences and meetings considering the role that some extended family members play in the educating of children?

5.3 REFLECTION QUESTIONS

1. What practices do you engage in that may undermine your relationship with some minority families (e.g., only have materials in one language)?
2. In what ways may your defensiveness or denial about racial problems within your school be alienating minority parents?
3. What developmental stage of cultural competence are you? Why is that? Does your current developmental stage impact the relationship you have with families?

SUMMARY

Building capacity of those who work with diverse families requires a reimagining of family support and engagement that meets the needs and strengths of minority families. This will require adjustments in practices and policies. Programs, schools, practitioners, and all those working with families for the benefit of children's learning and development will need to focus on expanding the traditional, one-way, directional approach of "family engagement" to a more culturally responsive, antibias bidirectional approach that sees families as valuable to the process of educating children, both because of their fundamental importance to children's growth and learning and because their engagement with programs matters in achieving current measures of accountability and success. Leaders and educators will also need to ensure that their practices are culturally relevant, reflective of families' race and ethnicity, as well as their economic and social conditions. This could lead not only to a focus on parent engagement in school-based programming, but also a focus on supporting engagement and empowerment in the home and community. Cultural competence is not, of course, mastered through one-day trainings, nor is it an added programmatic component. It needs, rather, to be integrated into all aspects of professional development, curriculum, assessment, and evaluation. It is a developmental process ranging from cultural destructiveness (e.g., negative policies or practices toward a particular group, such genocide) to cultural proficiency (e.g., attitudes and practices that values diversity) that requires proactiveness, intentionality, and authenticity.

In this book, we don't try to provide solutions and answers to all questions regarding, building cultural competence but rather provide, a culturally responsive, antibiased framework for family engagement. We believe use of this framework would strengthen practitioners, schools, and organizations, collaboration and partnership with diverse families.

REFERENCES

Aud, S., Fox, M. A., & KewalRamani, A. (2010). *Status and trends in the education of racial and ethnic groups (NCES 2010–015)*. Washington, DC: U.S. Department of Education, National Center for Education Statistics. U.S. Government Printing Office.

Avellar, S., Paulsell, D., Sama-Miller, E., & Grosso, P. D. (2012). *Home visiting evidence of effectiveness review*. Washington, DC: U.S. Department of Health and Human Services, Administration for Children and Families, Office of Planning, Research and Evaluation.

Bierman, A. (2006). Does religion buffer the effects of discrimination on mental health? Differing effects by race. *Journal for the Scientific Study of Religion, 45*(4), 551–565. Available from http://dx.doi.org/doi:10.1111/j.1468-5906.2006.00327.x.

Boethel, M. (2003). *Diversity: School, family, & community connections. Annual synthesis 2003*. Austin, TX: National Center for Family and Community Connections with Schools. Southwest Education Development Laboratory.

Brooks-Gunn, J., & Markman, L. B. (2005). The contribution of parenting to ethnic and racial gaps in school readiness. *The Future of Children, 15*(1), 139–168.

Burton, L. M., & Dilworth-Anderson, P. (1991). The intergenerational family roles of aged Black Americans. *Marriage and Family Review, 16*(3–4), 311–330. Available from http://dx.doi.org/doi:10.1300/J002v16n03_06.

Camarota, S. A. (2012). *Immigrants in the United States: A profile of American's foreign-born population*. Washington, DC: Center for Immigration Studies.

Camarota, S. A., & Jensenius, K. (2009). *A shifting tide: Recent trends in the illegal immigrant population (Backgrounder)*. Washington, DC: Center for Immigration Studies.

Caughy, M. O., O'Campo, P. J., & Muntaner, C. (2004). Experiences of racism among African American parents and the mental health of their preschool-aged children. *American Journal of Public Health, 94*, 2118–2124.

Caughy, M. O., O'Campo, P. J., Randolph, S. M., & Nickerson, K. (2002). The influence of racial socialization on practices on the cognitive and behavior competence of African American preschoolers. *Child Development, 73*, 1611–1625.

Child Care Services Association (2013). *T.E.A.C.H. Early childhood and child care wages annual national program report, 2012–2013*. Chapel Hill, NC: Child Care Services Association.

Chow, J. C., Jaffee, K., & Snowden, L. (2003). Racial/ethnic disparities in the use of mental health services in poverty areas. *American Journal of Public Health, 93*(5), 792–797. Available from http://dx.doi.org/doi:10.2105/ajph.93.5.792.

Conger, R. D., Conger, K. J., Elder, G. H., Lorenz, F. O., Simons, R. L., & Whitbeck, L. B. (1992). A family process model of economic hardship and adjustment of early adolescent boys. *Child Development, 63*(3), 526–541. Available from http://dx.doi.org/doi:10.1111/j.1467-8624.1992.tb01644.x.

Conger, R. D., Ge, X., Elder, G. H., Lorenz, F. O., & Simons, R. L. (1994). Economic stress, coercive family process, and developmental problems of adolescents. *Child Development, 65*(2), 541–561. Available from http://dx.doi.org/doi:10.1111/j.1467-8624.1994.tb00768.x.

Costello, E. J., Keeler, G. P., & Angold, A. (2001). Poverty, race/ethnicity, and psychiatric disorder. *American Journal of Public Health, 91*(9), 1494–1498.

Cross, T. L., Bazron, B. J., Dennis, K. W., & Isaacs, M. R. (1989). *Towards a culturally competent system of care (Vol. 1)*. Washington, DC: Child and Adolescent Service System Program Technical Assistance Center.

Curenton, S. M., & Iruka, I. U. (2013). *Cultural competence in early childhood education*. San Diego, CA: Bridgepoint Education, Inc.

Currie, J. M. (2005). Health disparities and gaps in school readiness. *The Future of Children, 15* (1), 117–138. Available from http://dx.doi.org/doi:10.1353/foc.2005.0002.

DeNavas-Walt, C., Proctor, B. D., & Smith, J. C. (2013). *U.S. Census Bureau, current population reports, P60-245, income, poverty, and health insurance coverage in the United States: 2012*. Washington, DC: U.S. Government Printing Office.

Diller, J. V., & Moule, J. (2005). *Cultural competence: A primer for educators*. Belmont, CA: Thomas Wadsworth.

Epstein, J. L., & Dauber, S. L. (1991). School programs and teacher practices of parent Involvement in inner-city elementary and middle schools. *The Elementary School Journal, 91*(3), 289–305.

Ewing, W. A. (2012). *Opportunity and exclusion: A brief history of U.S. Immigration Policy*. Washington, DC: American Immigration Council, Immigration Policy Center.

Feistritzer, E. C. (2011). *Profiles of teachers in the U.S. 2011*. Washington, DC: National Center for Education Information.

Fiscella, K., Franks, P., Gold, M. R., & Clancy, C. M. (2000). Inequality in quality: Addressing socioeconomic, racial, and ethnic disparities in health care. *JAMA, 283*(19), 2579–2584. Available from http://dx.doi.org/doi:10.1001/jama.283.19.2579.

Fuligni, A. J., Tseng, V., & Lam, M. (1999). Attitudes toward family obligations among American adolescents with Asian, Latin American, and European backgrounds. *Child Development, 70*(4), 1030–1044. Available from http://dx.doi.org/doi:10.2307/1132260.

Gartrell, N., & Bos, H. (2010). US National Longitudinal Lesbian Family Study: Psychological adjustment of 17-year-old adolescents. *Pediatrics, 126*(1), 28–36. Available from http://dx.doi.org/doi:10.1542/peds.2009-3153.

Gary, L. E. (1995). African American men's perceptions of racial discrimination: A sociocultural analysis. *Social Work Research, 19*(4), 207–217.

Gillanders, C., Iruka, I. U., Ritchie, S., & Cobb, C. (2012). Restructuring and aligning early education opportunities for cultural, language and ethnic minority children. In R. Pianta, S. Barnett, L. Justice, & S. Sheridan (Eds.), *Handbood of early education* (pp. 111–136). New York, NY: Guilford Publications, Inc.

Golombok, S., Perry, B., Burston, A., Murray, C., Mooney-Somers, J., Stevens, M., et al. (2003). Children with lesbian parents: A community study. *Developmental Psychology, 39*(1), 20–33. Available from http://dx.doi.org/doi:10.1037/0012-1649.39.1.20.

Han, J. (2007). Triumphs of Title IX. *Ms Magazine,* 42–47.

Harden, A. W., Clark, R. L., & Maguire, K. (1997). *Informal and formal kinship care*. Washington, DC: U.S. Department of Health and Human Services.

Hill, N. E. (2001). Parenting and academic socialization as they relate to school readiness: The roles of ethnicity and family income. *Journal of Educational Psychology, 93*(4), 686–697. Available from http://dx.doi.org/doi:10.1037/0022-0663.93.4.686.

Hogg, L. (2011). Funds of knowledge: An investigation of coherence within the literature. *Teaching and Teacher Education, 27*(3), 666–677. doi: <http://dx.doi.org/10.1016/j.tate.2010.11.005>.

Hughes, D., & Chen, L. (1997). When and what parents tell children about race: An examination of race-related socialization among African American families. *Applied Development Science, 1*, 200–214.

Hughes, D., & Chen, L. (1999). The nature of parents' race-related communications to children: A developmental perspective. In L. Balter, & C. S. Tamis-LeMonda (Eds.), Child psychology: A handbook of contemporary issues. Philadelphia: Psychology Press/Taylor & Francis.

Hughes, D. (2003). Correlates of African American and latino parents' messages to children about ethnicity and race: A comparative study of racial socialization. *American Journal of Community Psychology, 31*, 15−33.

Iruka, I. U. (2009). Ethnic variation in the association between family structure and practices on child outcomes at 36 months: Results from Early Head Start. *Early Education and Development, 20*(1), 148−173. Available from http://dx.doi.org/doi:10.1080/10409280802206916.

Iruka, I. U. (2013). *The black family: Re-imagining family support and engagement for children. Being black is not a risk factor: A strengths-based look at the state of the black child.* Washington, DC: National Black Child Development Institute.

Jeynes, W. H. (2003). The effects of black and hispanic 12th graders living in intact families and being religious on their academic achievement. *Urban Education January 2003, 38*(1), 35−57. Available from http://dx.doi.org/doi:10.1177/0042085902238685.

Joe, E. M., & Davis, J. E. (2009). Parental influence, school readiness and early academic achievement of African American boys. *The Journal of Negro Education, 78*(3), 260−276.

Livingston, G., & Parker, K. (2010). *Since the start of the great recession, more children raised by grandparents: A social & demographic trends report.* Washington, DC: Pew Research Center.

Mays, V. M., Cochran, S. D., & Barnes, N. W. (2006). Race, race-based discrimination, and health outcomes among African Americans. *Annual Review of Psychology, 58*(1), 201−225. Available from http://dx.doi.org/doi:10.1146/annurev.psych.57.102904.190212.

McKown, C., & Weinstein, R. S. (2008). Teacher expectations, classroom context, and the achievement gap. *Journal of School Psychology, 46*(3), 235−261. Available from http://dx.doi.org/doi:10.1016/j.jsp.2007.05.001.

McLanahan, S. S. (1983). Family structure and stress: A longitudinal comparison of two-parent and female-headed families. *Journal of Marriage and Family, 45*(2), 347−357. Available from http://dx.doi.org/doi:10.2307/351513.

McLoyd, V. C. (1990). The impact of economic hardship on Black families and children: Psychological distress, parenting, and socioemotional development. *Child Development, 61*(2), 311−346. Available from http://dx.doi.org/doi:10.1111/j.1467-8624.1990.tb02781.x.

McWayne, C., Hampton, V., Fantuzzo, J., Cohen, H. L., & Sekino, Y. (2004). A multivariate examination of parent involvement and the social and academic competencies of urban kindergarten children. *Psychology in the Schools, 41*(3), 363−377.

Mendez, J. L. (2010). How can parents get involved in preschool? Barriers and engagement in education by ethnic minority parents of children attending Head Start. *Cultural Diversity and Ethnic Minority Psychology, 16*(1), 26−36. Available from http://dx.doi.org/doi:10.1037/a0016258.

Moll, L. C., & Greenberg, J. B. (1990). Creating zones of possibilities: Combining social contexts for instruction. In L. C. Moll (Ed.), *Vygotsky and education: Instructional implications and applications of sociohistorical psychology* (pp. 319−348). Cambridge: Cambridge University Press.

Movement Advancement Project (2011). *All children matter: How legal and social inequities hurt LGBT families.* Denver, CO: Author.

Ong, A. D., Fuller-Rowell, T., & Burrow, A. L. (2009). Racial discrimination and the stress process. *Journal of Personality and Social Psychology, 96*(6), 1259−1271. Available from http://dx.doi.org/doi:10.1037/a0015335.

Parker, F. L., Boak, A. Y., Griffin, K. W., Ripple, C., & Peay, L. (1999). Parent−child relationship, home learning environment, and school readiness. *School Psychology Review, 28*(3), 413−425.

Parker, K., & Wang, W. (2013). *Modern parenthood: Roles of moms and dads converge as they balance work and family*. Washington, DC: Pew Research Center.

Pungello, E. P., Iruka, I. U., Dotterer, A. M., Mills-Koonce, R., & Reznick, J. S. (2009). The effects of socioeconomic status, race, and parenting on language development in early childhood. *Developmental Psychology, 45*(2), 544–557. Available from http://dx.doi.org/doi:10.1037/a0013917.

Riolo, S. A., Nguyen, T. A., Greden, J. F., & King, C. A. (2005). Prevalence of depression by race/ethnicity: Findings from the National Health and Nutrition Examination Survey III. *American Journal of Public Health, 95*(6), 998–1000. Available from http://dx.doi.org/doi:10.2105/ajph.2004.047225.

Rodgers, W. (2008). Understanding the Black–White earnings gap. Retrieved from <http://prospect.org/article/understanding-black-white-earnings-gap>.

Sarkisian, N., Gerena, M., & Gerstel, N. (2006). Extended family ties among Mexicans, Puerto Ricans, and Whites: Superintegration or disintegration? *Family Relations, 55*(3), 331–344. Available from http://dx.doi.org/doi:10.1111/j.1741-3729.2006.00408.x.

Spencer, M. B., & Markstrom-Adams, C. (1990). Identity processes among racial and ethnic minority children in America. *Child Development, 61*(2), 290–310. Available from http://dx.doi.org/doi:10.2307/1131095.

Suizzo, M., Robinson, C., & Pahlke, E. (2009). African American mothers' socialization beliefs and goals with young children: Themes of history, education, and collective independence. *Journal of Family Issues, 29*, 287–316.

Steffen, P. R., & Bowden, M. (2006). Sleep disturbance mediates the relationship between perceived racism and depressive symptoms. *Ethnicity and Disease, 16*, 16–21.

Taveras, E. M., Gillman, M. W., Kleinman, K., Rich-Edwards, J. W., & Rifas-Shiman, S. L. (2010). Racial/ethnic differences in early-life risk factors for childhood obesity. *Pediatrics, 125*(4), 686–695. Available from http://dx.doi.org/doi:10.1542/peds.2009-2100.

U.S. Bureau of the Census, C. S. S. U. C. C. S. (2001). *Census 2000 supplementary survey profile for California*. Washington, DC: U.S. Bureau of the Census.

U.S. Department of Education, N. C. f. E. S. (2007). *The condition of education 2007 (NCES 2007–064)*. Washington, DC: U.S. Government Printing Office.

U.S. Department of Justice (2012). *Equal access to education: Forty years of Title IX*. Washington, DC: U.S. Department of Justice.

Uttal, L. (1999). Using kin for child care: Embedment in the socioeconomic networks of extended families. *Journal of Marriage and Family, 61*(4), 845–857. Available from http://dx.doi.org/doi:10.2307/354007.

Wang, Y., & Beydoun, M. A. (2007). The obesity epidemic in the United States—gender, age, socioeconomic, racial/ethnic, and geographic characteristics: A systematic review and meta-regression analysis. *Epidemiologic Reviews, 29*(1), 6–28. Available from http://dx.doi.org/doi:10.1093/epirev/mxm007.

Whittman, P., & Velde, B. P. (2002). Attaining cultural competence, critical thinking, and intellectual development: A challenge for occupational therapists. *The American Journal of Occupational Therapy, 56*(4), 454–456.